SIMPLY
LENT

SIMPLY LENT

A JOURNEY OF REFLECTION AND RENEWAL WITH JESUS

LISA FAHEY

For information on distribution rights, royalties, derivative works, or licensing opportunities on behalf of this content or work, please get in touch with the publisher at the address below:

Farmhouse Publishings, LLC
P.O. Box 333
Spearfish, SD 57783

Although the author and publisher have tried to ensure that the information and advice in this book were correct and accurate at press time, the author and publisher do not assume and disclaim any liability to any party for any loss, damage, or disruption caused by acting upon the information in this book or by errors or omissions, whether such errors or omissions result from negligence, accident, or any other cause.

ISBN (Softcover): 979-8-9918470-4-9
ISBN (Ebook): 979-8-9918470-5-6

Design by Heidi Caperton
Editing by Kendra Paulton

Printed in the United States of America.

To my husband, Pat— the one who listened to God on the day of Shane's accident. When He said, *"Take care of Lisa,"* you obeyed without knowing what that would mean. To this day, every Lent, you remind me of the significance of saying *yes* to God. I am forever grateful for your faithfulness, love, and unwavering support. Thank you for answering His call. I love and appreciate you dearly.

Table of Contents

Have you ever felt a strong calling to do something but chose to ignore it? That's how I've felt about writing on the topic of Lent. Despite my numerous excuses for putting it off, I believe this project represents one of the most urgent calls to action I've ever received. Allow me to share a few reasons for my hesitation:

- Seasonal Gloom: Lent occurs in the winter, a time that's inherently marked by a sense of gloom.
- Pious Temptations: There's often a tendency to approach Lent with an air of piety—focusing on what we're giving up or publicly sharing our acts of almsgiving and penance.
- Personal Grief: Perhaps the most significant reason for my reluctance is that I lost my first husband just before Ash Wednesday forty years ago.

Reflecting on this, I recalled a blog post I wrote a couple of years ago titled "No Doom or Gloom This Lenten Season." A few years ago in church, Fr. Jonathan remarked, "We do not have to approach Lent with doom and gloom." To be candid, Lent has never been my favorite liturgical season. As I read my friends' posts about their resolutions for approaching Lent, I often find myself in a very different place.

On February 19, 1985, my first husband was killed in a horse accident; the following day marked Ash Wednesday and the beginning of Lent.

During this tumultuous time in my life, I experienced my own "Paschal Mystery:"

- Death: I felt a profound loss—dying to the life I thought I would lead.
- The Tomb: I encountered grief, loneliness, and fear, much like being in a tomb.
- The Resurrection: It was within this 'tomb' that I received a touching card from my Great Aunt, Sister Anna Rose. While she sympathized with me, she also provided encouragement—she urged me not to remain in that dark place for too long. Here is an excerpt from the note she sent me:

"My dearest Lisa, I am so sorry to hear about your husband, Shane. It's truly remark-able to have known a young man that God called home so soon—He must have had an important job for Shane in Heaven. It's okay to feel sadness and to cry for a while, but

then you must rise and serve the Lord. Know that you are in my thoughts and prayers. All my love, Sister Anna Rose."

The third part of the Paschal Mystery—Resurrection—was made possible through the truth and encouragement embedded in my great aunt's words. They provided me with the courage to step toward God's plans for me.

A few years ago, I finally understood why Lent has been difficult for me. I realized that God wasn't inviting me to dwell in gloom and doom but rather to draw closer to Him. Consequently, I choose to embrace Fr. Jonathan's advice and approach the Lenten season with a mindset of joy as I pray, fast, and support those in need. The essence of Lent is to draw nearer to Jesus, who has already made the ultimate sacrifice.

After dedicating time to prayer, I had sensed a call to write *Simply Lent*. My aim is to keep the approach uncomplicated, reminiscent of my previous works, *Simply Advent* and my Bible studies. During Lent, we're invited to shed what no longer serves us and to make room for new life. Each day, we'll draw on the virtues to aid in this transformative process.

I do not intend to cause emotions of gloom or guilt. Rather, I aspire to establish an orderly balance that encourages authentic encounters with God and His Son, Jesus.

May this season lead you ever closer to the heart of Jesus as you anticipate the hope of Easter.

Lisa

INSTRUCTIONS

Lent is a beautiful season filled with moments of reflection, heartfelt repentance, and a chance to renew our spirits. It serves as a divine invitation, calling us to embark on an introspective journey that allows us to examine our lives more closely. During this sacred season of Lent, I warmly invite you to delve into the virtues that encourage a candid exploration of our weaknesses—those aspects of ourselves that may hinder our spiritual growth. By confronting these vulnerabilities, we can arm ourselves with the tools necessary to overcome them, molding us into the individuals that God has always envisioned us to be—transformed, renewed, and filled with purpose.

Lent is not merely a time of sacrifice; it is an opportunity to cultivate resilience, compassion, and a profound understanding of ourselves. It is in this season that we can dismantle the barriers preventing us from fully embracing God's love and grace.

Alongside these reflections, I encourage you to engage in meaningful calls to action—simple yet impactful gestures that resonate with the core of the Lenten spirit. Whether it is reaching out to those in need, performing acts of kindness, or simply taking a moment each day for quiet contemplation, these actions can deepen your understanding of love and service, mirroring the life of Jesus.

In addition, I invite you to carve out sacred moments of prayer, where your spirit can connect intimately with the Divine. Prayer can be a transformative experience, a quiet conversation that soothes the soul and clarifies the mind. These moments will help you to center your thoughts and open your heart, preparing you for the joyous celebrations that await us at Easter.

As you engage with these journaling prompts, let each word be a step closer in your journey towards Jesus. Allow them to invite you into a deeper relationship with Him, illuminating the path that leads to a heart brimming with joyful anticipation for the upcoming celebrations of Easter.

I've included a QR code that links to a *Simply Lent* playlist on Spotify—enjoy the music as you walk through Lent! You'll also find a QR code for the Leader's Guide right next to the playlist.

May this sacred season gently draw you closer to the loving heart of Jesus. Let it nurture your spirit and prepare you for the joyous hope and renewal that Easter embodies. Embrace these reflections, actions, and prayers as sacred gifts, and let them guide you to a place of peace, renewal, and transformation.

SIMPLY LENT - SPOTIFY PLAYLIST

SCAN ME!

@LISA FAHEY MINISTRY - WWW.LISAFAHEY.COM

LISA FAHEY MINISTRY - LEADERS GUIDE

SCAN ME!

@LISAFAHEYMINISTRY / WWW.LISAFAHEY.COM

ASH WEDNESDAY REFLECTIONS

ALMSGIVING, PRAYER, AND FASTING

T he perfect way to begin Lent is by having a clear understanding of the call to action of almsgiving, prayer, and fasting. Almsgiving, prayer, and fasting are to express a conversion in relation to oneself, to God, and to others.[1] The best place to start is Matthew 6:1-18.

In Matthew 6, Jesus emphasizes the importance of sincerity in our actions, particularly in doing good deeds, praying, and fasting. He instructs His followers not to perform these acts for the purpose of being seen by others or to gain their approval. Instead, Jesus teaches that genuine acts of righteousness should be done in secret, where only God sees and rewards them.

This sermon challenges the motivation behind our good deeds. It warns against the hypocrisy of performing acts of kindness or spirituality for the sake of public recognition, rather than from a place of true faith and devotion. Essentially, Jesus argues that the intention behind our actions is crucial; they should stem from a desire to serve God and not from the desire for human praise or recognition.

In doing so, Jesus redefines what it means to live a righteous life, encouraging a focus on inner virtue over outward appearances. This principle emphasizes humility and authenticity in our spiritual practices and interpersonal relationships.

Let's look to Matthew 6:1-4 regarding almsgiving.

[But] take care not to perform righteous deeds in order that people may see them; otherwise, you will have no recompense from your heavenly Father. When you give alms, do not blow a trumpet before you, as the hypocrites do in the synagogues and in the streets to win the praise of others. Amen, I say to you, they have received their reward. But when you give alms, do not let your left hand know what your right is doing, so that your almsgiving may be secret. And your Father who sees in secret will repay you.

Almsgiving invites us to shift our focus from our own desires to the needs of others. It's an opportunity to give a part of ourselves, to step outside of our personal wants, and make a meaningful difference in the lives of those around us.

Let me share an example from my own journey. A few seasons ago, I felt a strong calling during Lent to take a vow of simplicity. I committed to purchasing only groceries and basic necessities—no new clothes, no decorative items for the home. I would only purchase the absolute bare minimum. This wasn't always easy! With the world at our fingertips and the convenience of online shopping, it was a real challenge to resist the urge to splurge with just a click online.

But this intentional choice led to something beautiful. Instead, the money I would have spent on those seasonal items went toward a local charity that serves our community. By giving up a little, I found a way to give so much more. In letting go of my cravings for new things, I was able to invest in the lives of others, highlighting the profound impact we can make when we prioritize helping those in need.

Almsgiving might require sacrifice, but it opens our hearts to generosity and teaches us that true fulfillment often lies in giving rather than receiving. This Lent, I encourage you to consider how you, too, can invite this spirit of giving into your life. What can you forgo in order to uplift someone else? The blessing of generosity awaits!

Now we will take a look at prayer found in Matthew 6:5-15:

When you pray, do not be like the hypocrites, who love to stand and pray in the synagogues and on street corners so that others may see them. Amen, I say to you, they have received their reward. But when you pray, go to your inner room, close the door, and pray to your Father in secret. And your Father who sees in secret will repay you. In praying, do not babble like the pagans, who think that they will be heard because of their many words. Do not be like them. Your Father knows what you need before you ask him.

"This is how you are to pray: Our Father in heaven, hallowed be your name, your kingdom come, your will be done, on earth as in heaven. Give us today our daily bread; and forgive us our debts, as we forgive our debtors; and do not subject us to the final test, but

deliver us from the evil one. If you forgive others their transgressions, your heavenly Father will forgive you. But if you do not forgive others, neither will your Father forgive your transgressions.

Prayer is one of the most precious gifts God has given us—a direct line of communication with our Creator. It's not just about words; it's a deep, meaningful conversation between the Almighty and ourselves. When we approach prayer with a heart and mind attuned to His magnificence, grace, and sovereignty, we cultivate a spirit of humility that opens the door to genuinely connecting with Him.

Many people find prayer challenging, and often, this struggle stems from not making it a regular part of our daily lives. Like any meaningful relationship, our connection with God flourishes when we invest time. When we carve out moments to sit quietly with Jesus each day, we discover that prayer flows more naturally.

An excellent place to start is with the prayer He taught us—*The Lord's Prayer.* Take each line to heart, reflecting on its meaning, and then let your words spill out, sharing what's on your mind and heart. Remember, God already knows every detail of your life; He simply longs for you to trust Him enough to share it all—the joys, the struggles, and everything in between.

Embrace this divine gift of prayer. It's an opportunity to deepen your relationship with God, to speak freely, and to listen earnestly. Allow your conversations with Him to become a comforting habit that enriches your spirit and draws you closer to His heart.

Now let's take a look at fasting that can be found in Matthew 6:16-18:

When you fast, do not look gloomy like the hypocrites. They neglect their appearance, so that they may appear to others to be fasting. Amen, I say to you, they have received their reward. But when you fast, anoint your head and wash your face, so that you may not appear to others to be fasting, except to your Father who is hidden. And your Father who sees what is hidden will repay you.

Fasting is a fascinating concept with a wealth of teachings surrounding its purpose and benefits. From enhancing our ability to hear God's voice more clearly to improving our digestive health, fasting offers diverse insights into our lives. Whether you're already familiar with fasting or just starting to explore it, I want to share a simple yet powerful principle for considering fasting this Lent.

Many of us are accustomed to the idea of giving up treats like coffee, wine, or sweets during this season. However, I encourage you to think outside the box, contemplate fasting from certain luxuries or indulgences, and focus on being self-disciplined instead. For instance, if you're often late, consider fasting from that habit by striving to be on time for the next 40 days. Alternatively, if you frequently treat yourself to a manicure, why not choose to skip it this Lent? These are just a couple of examples that can help you connect with the true essence of fasting.

Lent is a profound time for spiritual growth—it invites us to deepen our connection with God. By intentionally stepping back from certain foods or habits, we create a space for reflection, prayer, and a reassessment of our priorities. Ultimately, fasting during Lent isn't just about what we give up; it's about opening our hearts and drawing closer to God in the process.

This is a season to embrace wholeheartedly, allowing it to transform us as we engage more deeply with our spirituality. Reflect on how fasting, combined with prayer and acts of charity, can lead you into a more intimate relationship with Jesus. As you meditate on these questions, take the opportunity to approach Lent with anticipation and a willingness to grow.

How can these acts deepen your faith and strengthen your resolve?

What is one habit or mindset you feel God is calling you to change during this season?

How can you use this Scripture to intercede for others in prayer?

HUMILITY

In the previous chapter on Ash Wednesday, it was stated that sincere prayer demands humility. This raises the question: why not begin by addressing one of the most challenging obstacles for most of us—humility itself? What makes it difficult is that humility means taking our attention off of ourselves and our importance. Essentially, it requires us to recognize and prioritize others instead of constantly thinking about ourselves.

From the moment I wake up, my mind revisits conversations from the day before—some of them pleasant, others a bit tense. Whether it's something I said or something someone said to me, I tend to assume it's all directed at me. My mind starts imagining all sorts of negative things people might be thinking about me. As a result, I find myself stuck in a loop of self-absorption.

> *Sincere prayer demands humility.*

The Merriam-Webster dictionary defines *humility* as "freedom from pride or arrogance." Furthermore, *humility* means "the state of being humble." *Humble* is defined as "not proud or haughty, not arrogant or assertive." Humble originates from the Latin word *humilis*, meaning "low."[2] For many, the lowness in humility is worth cultivating.

When we think of the story of salvation, we start in the Garden of Eden. God created everything excellent and beautiful. He created angels, and these angels were knowledgeable beings. One of the angels who had the highest rank would not submit himself to God. He wanted to be above God; therefore, he had an issue with humility. Satan tempted Adam and Eve to shift their reliance from God to themselves. As a result, they were banished from the Garden of Eden for disobeying God. Similarly, Lucifer, once known as the angel of light, was cast out of the garden due to his pride, along with other angels who also struggled with humility.

This one story of a lack of humility changed the course of the world. Because of this, the perfect relationship between God and humanity was broken. But God, in His infinite love, set a plan of redemption into motion. He sent His Son, Jesus, to reconcile us and bring us back to Him.

The opposite of humility is pride. Pride is one of the seven deadly sins. Pride means thinking of ourselves more and others less. You see, if all we do is think about ourselves, we will be entangled in the deadly sin of pride.

I remember being in a sales training once, and the speaker said, "If you think everyone is thinking about what you are doing or saying, you are wrong; they are too busy thinking about themselves." So don't worry about what people are doing, for they have their own worries and problems of their own.

Here is a quote by Rick Warren from his book *The Purpose Driven Life*: "Humility is not thinking less of yourself, it is thinking of yourself, less."[3] In other words, humility is thinking of others more and ourselves less.

TAKE TIME TO:

- Take a few minutes each day to reflect on situations where pride may have influenced your thoughts or actions, journal your experiences, and focus on shifting your perspective to think more about others.
- Engage in weekly acts of kindness or service, such as helping colleagues or friends in need, to practice humility and foster a mindset of generosity and selflessness. This can be as simple as offering a helping hand.

SCRIPTURE VERSES TO READ & REFLECT:

- Ephesians 4:2-3
- Luke 14:11
- Romans 12:16

MY PRAYER FOR TODAY

WEEKEND REFLECTION

A TIME TO REFLECT AND SURRENDER

As we approach this sacred season of Lent, we find ourselves at a significant crossroads. Lent is a time to pause and reflect on our hearts and our relationship with God. This season offers each of us a beautiful opportunity to draw closer to Him, relinquish the burdens that weigh us down, and embrace a greater trust in God's divine plans for our lives.

When we reflect on the story of Jesus being tempted in the wilderness (Matthew 4:1–11), we are reminded that even in our darkest moments and times of trial, we can find strength and purpose. The season of Lent invites us into a space of surrender—an invitation to let go of control, fears, anxieties, and distractions that may keep us from experiencing the fullness of God's love.

In our journey through life, when we pause to acknowledge the countless blessings surrounding us, we unveil a profound truth about God's unwavering presence. The divine grace intricately interwoven into our experiences can be seen in each moment of gratitude. By allowing our hearts and minds to be open, we become receptive to the subtle whispers of the Holy Spirit, which provide us with wisdom and love. These gentle nudges remind us to reflect deeply and contemplate the landscapes of our emotions and thoughts. In this sacred space of reflection and connection, we find clarity and a renewed sense of purpose, allowing God's light to shine through us and illuminate the path ahead. Let us embrace this journey with faith, knowing that we are never alone and that every step we take is a testament to His endless love.

I encourage you to set aside intentional moments for journaling your innermost thoughts, prayers, and reflections. As you journal, invite the Holy Spirit to guide your thoughts and open your heart to God's presence. In these quiet moments, seek the Holy Spirit's enlightenment on your heart—what areas may need your surrender? Where might God be inviting you to trust Him more deeply?

Embrace the themes of reflection and surrender this Lent, confident that as we grow closer to Him, we will experience a profound sense of serenity, renewed strength, and hope. May this be a time of spiritual growth where we become more attuned to God's love and purpose in our lives.

QUESTIONS FOR REFLECTION:

What burdens or distractions am I holding onto that may be keeping me from fully experiencing God's love?

In what ways have I experienced God's presence in my life, and how can I cultivate gratitude for these moments?

What fears or uncertainties do I need to surrender to God, trusting in His divine plan for my life?

LOVE THY NEIGHBOR

As we discovered in the last lesson on humility, we should be more mindful of others. "Love thy neighbor" has a pleasant sound to it, but it isn't always easy, right?

The Bible emphasizes the importance of loving your neighbor as yourself, which involves sacrifice, compassion, justice, forgiveness, sharing, love for God, reaching out to God's children, and sharing a meal. These acts of love not only show love for God but also fulfill the deepest meaning of who we are.

I love the neighborhood where we live because everyone keeps an eye out for one another. Honestly, it was only a few years ago that I knew only our neighbors' names, but I didn't know anything about them. We would share a wave, a hello, or a smile, but that was it.

Ennie Hickman, a former youth minister and the founder of Del Rey Collective and Adore, recounted how he and his wife, Cana, chose to invite their neighbors to their home for food and fellowship. They aimed to strengthen their relationships with their neighbors and share the Good News of Christ with them. After hearing about their outreach efforts, God inspired me to connect more with our neighbors.

Last summer, one of my neighbors organized a gathering to celebrate our birthdays, and she suggested we meet once a month. Since then, the women on our block have been getting together monthly. We alternate hosting one another at our houses, attending community events, or celebrating milestones, like someone's cancer recovery. We also have enjoyed going to sip-and-paint classes together.

Getting to know these women has been incredibly rewarding. I've learned about their victories, struggles, and backgrounds. While there are some neighbors with whom it's challenging to connect, we've all committed to praying for them and waiting for guidance on how to best support them.

TAKE TIME TO:

- Ponder on what ways God is calling you to love your neighbor more.
- Engage in monthly neighborhood check-ins to catch up, offer support, and pray for each other's needs, strengthening relationships and allowing you to provide assistance when needed.

SCRIPTURE VERSES TO READ AND REFLECT:

- Matthew 22:36-40
- Mark 12:28-34
- 1 John 4:20-21

MY PRAYER FOR TODAY

POVERTY OF SPIRIT

Poverty of spirit embodies a complete reliance on God. In *The Ignatian Adventure* by Kevin O'Brien, SJ, it is noted that "poverty of spirit is an emptying of self so that God can fill us with life and love."[4] This profound concept invites us to reflect on the idea of utter dependence. The term "utter" conveys absolute reliance, indicating that we surrender any sense of independence. "Dependence" suggests that we lean entirely on someone else for support and fulfillment.

I often find myself wanting to control various aspects of my life—my children, my health, and even the opinions of others about me. However, embracing poverty of spirit calls me to trust that God, as the Creator of all, desires only the best for us. It is through this surrender of control that we create space to receive God's love.

> *It is through this surrender of control that we create space to receive God's love.*

A poignant reminder comes to mind: "You cannot give what you do not have." We cannot share God's love with others unless we first acknowledge our complete dependence on Him to support us and meet our needs. By allowing ourselves to be emptied and filled with His love, we become vessels of His grace in the world.

Our vulnerabilities are not indicators of weakness but invitations to grow closer to God. They remind us that in our emptiness, His fullness awaits. It is important to embrace letting go. Letting go of our sense of control and self-sufficiency, we expose our hearts to the transformative power of His love. From this divine interaction—our humility to His abundance—true strength results. Each act of trust we perform demonstrates the extent of our dependence on Him.

As we arrange our days, may we seek periods of solitude to hear His voice and ask Him to dwell in the areas where we feel inadequate. By doing this, we become living models of His grace and expose His love to a society often seeking hope.

TAKE TIME TO:

- In what areas of your life do you feel challenged to let go of control and embrace a deeper reliance on God's love and guidance?
- How can practicing poverty of spirit transform your relationships and enable you to better share God's love with those around you?

SCRIPTURE VERSES TO READ AND REFLECT:

- Matthew 5:3
- Isaiah 61:1
- Isaiah 66:2

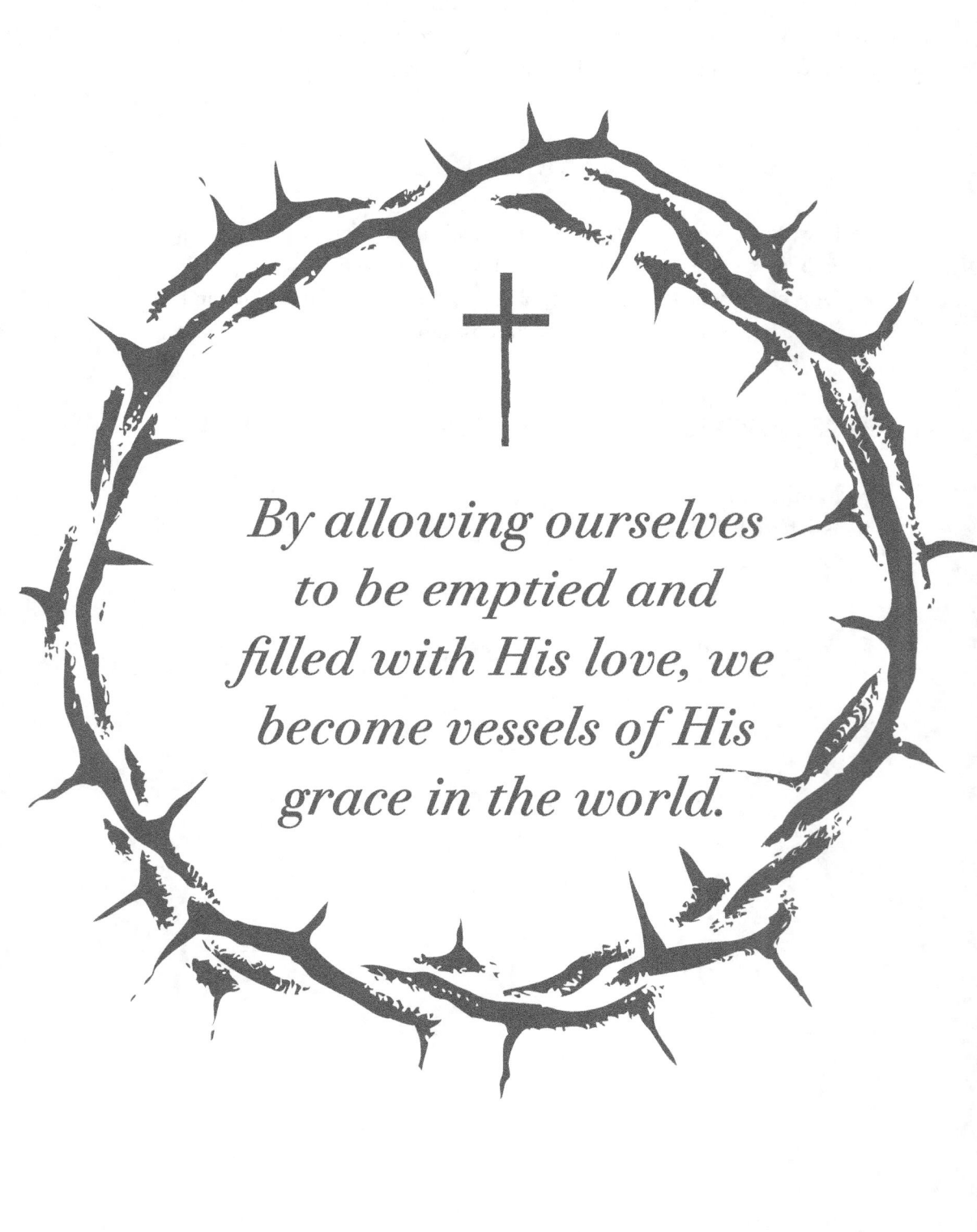

By allowing ourselves to be emptied and filled with His love, we become vessels of His grace in the world.

MY PRAYER FOR TODAY

OBEDIENCE

When we initially view obedience through the lens of human experience, we may perceive it as a hardship or a compromise of our freedom. As I struggle with my pride and need for independence, my first instinct is usually resistance. The concept of obedience contradicts my natural need to express my independence. However, this initial emotion is quickly overshadowed by a deeper understanding of what obedience truly means in the context of our faith.

As I reflect on the significance of obeying God, I recognize that it is rooted not in restriction, but in love. God, in His infinite wisdom, has laid out guidelines—the Ten Commandments—for our lives through His Word, not to constrain us, but to set us free. The commandments serve as guardrails, designed to protect us from the pitfalls of life. When I embrace obedience, I align myself with God's plan and tap into His desires for my life.

Choosing obedience does not mean that obstacles will not arise in daily life. Rather, it means facing life's obstacles with clarity and purpose. By deciding to submit to His authority, we discover the serenity that results from living in line with God's will, not the absence of adversity.

As I lean into obedience, I appreciate the beauty of yielding to God's authority. Each obedient choice propels me forward on my spiritual journey, enabling me to trust Him more deeply. His commands aren't mere suggestions but invitations to experience His blessings and joy in our lives.

On days when I struggle with obedience, I will pause to remind myself of this fundamental truth: God only wants the very best for me. I create room for mercy, direction, and fulfillment that comes from living in line with His ways by choosing to submit to His authority. Obedience is a path to a greater, more meaningful life, not an obligation. We are invited to rise above our pride and foster a heart willing to comply, surrendering our will to the One who understands us best. May we embrace this path with a heart ready to cooperate, giving our will to the One who knows us most.

TAKE TIME TO

- Reflect on ways to submit to God's authority in daily life, identify resistance areas, pray for strength, and choose obedience for experiencing God's blessings and peace.
- Engage in a week of intentional obedience, aligning your actions with God's Word.

SCRIPTURE VERSES TO READ AND REFLECT:

- Matthew 7:21
- John 14:15
- Psalm 112:1

MY PRAYER FOR TODAY

HONESTY

“It's just a little white lie.” How often have we used this phrase to justify bending the truth? These small untruths seem harmless, whether it's exaggerating a story, hiding a mistake, or telling someone what they want to hear to avoid conflict. But are they?

The term "little white lie" makes dishonesty appear insignificant—a lesser offense that doesn't really count. But God's Word doesn't categorize lies into "big" or "small." In Proverbs 12:22, we see that the Lord detests lying lips. It doesn't say He detests "big" lies more than "little" ones. To God, honesty and integrity are markers of a trustworthy heart.

Why do we tell "little white lies"? Often, it's to protect ourselves. We may not want to face the consequences of telling the truth or risk hurting someone's feelings. But even these seemingly noble intentions can lead us away from the heart of God. When we choose honesty, we prioritize others above our own comfort, trusting God to handle the fallout from the truth. When we justify telling white lies, they can begin to form a habit.

Think about Jesus, the epitome of honesty. He shared the truth with genuine love and compassion, regardless of its popularity. His unwavering dedication to truth revealed not only His integrity but also His profound love for others. He invites us, His followers, to embody that same commitment.

Honesty invites trust and builds stronger relationships. When we choose to speak truthfully, even in uncomfortable situations, we honor God and demonstrate love to others. Avoiding a small lie today might feel awkward, but it's a step toward deeper integrity and a clearer conscience before the Lord.

TAKE TIME TO

- How can you practice honesty in your daily interactions, even when it's uncomfortable?
- What would it look like to trust God with the outcomes of telling the truth?

SCRIPTURE VERSES TO READ AND REFLECT:

- Proverbs 12:22
- Colossians 3:9-10
- Ephesians 4:25

MY PRAYER FOR TODAY

THOUGHTS FOR THE WEEK

WEEKEND REFLECTION

REPENTANCE AND CONFESSION

Lent, preceded by the solemn observance of Ash Wednesday, is a sacred season for reflection and preparation for the journey toward Easter. It reminds us of our mortality and the fleeting nature of our earthly life. The words of Scripture, *For you are dust, and to dust you shall return* (Genesis 3:19 NABRE), capture our humble origins and inevitable return to the earth.

During Lent, we are encouraged to engage in deeper reflection, sincere confession, and a deliberate turning away from anything that distances us from God. This sacred season calls us to repentance, urging us to confront our shortcomings, acknowledge our faults, and sincerely seek the forgiveness we deeply need.

At the heart of Lent is a profound message: God longs for a renewed relationship with His creation. Christians trust that, through Jesus Christ's selfless love, they will one day be reunited with Him in the eternal embrace of Heaven. This journey of faith and reconciliation reminds us that, no matter our past, God always welcomes us back into His loving arms.

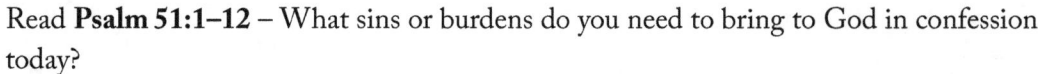

QUESTIONS FOR REFLECTION:

Read **Psalm 51:1–12** – What sins or burdens do you need to bring to God in confession today?

Read **Joel 2:12–13** – What does it mean to "return to the Lord with all your heart"?

How does this passage challenge you to examine areas where you've drifted from God?

REPENTANCE

Today, let's explore the beautiful and transformative topic of repentance. Repentance is about a change of heart—a turning away from sin and moving closer to God. It begins with a deep sense of sorrow for offending Him and leads to a transformation in our lives, accompanied by a commitment to walk away from sin and embrace His grace (CCC 1427-33).[5]

So often, when we hear someone's story or testimony, it revolves around a moment when they realized just how distant they felt from God. And then, something pivotal happened—a moment that transformed their heart and drew them toward Him. That's what repentance feels like. It's a shift that sparks a longing to change, to be better. You grieve over your sins and make the choice to strive for a better version of yourself. It's as if to say, "This is who I used to be, but because of Jesus, I'm becoming who He created me to be."

Just the other day, a friend asked me about my word for the new year. Honestly, I couldn't remember it at first. She smiled and said, "Well, I know you're always striving to be better." Her words made me pause. How did she see that in me? I told her that I try my best, but there are moments when I fail miserably. Following my conversion, I came to understand the importance of repentance—not as a one-time event but as a way of life. I've realized that when I fail, I can't wait to make it right. I need to turn to God immediately, ask for His forgiveness, and lean on Him to help me get back on track.

> *Repentance isn't about perfection; it's about persistence.*

Repentance isn't about perfection; it's about persistence. It's about taking one step at a time toward Him, trusting that He's there to catch you when you stumble, and celebrating the work He's doing in your heart and life.

TAKE TIME TO:

- Identify one tangible step you can take today to live out your repentance. It might be seeking forgiveness from someone, spending time in prayer, or letting go of a habit that pulls you away from God. Whatever it is, commit to it and trust that He will guide you on the path of change.
- Take a moment to reflect on your own journey. Is there an area of your life where you feel distant from God? Ask Him to reveal anything that needs repentance, and invite Him to transform your heart. Write down your thoughts and make it a priority to repent, trusting in God's great mercy.

SCRIPTURE VERSES TO READ AND REFLECT:

- Matthew 3:8
- 1 John 1:9
- Luke 5:31–32
- 2 Chronicles 7:14

*Repentance is about
a change of heart—a
turning away from
sin and moving
closer to God.*

MY PRAYER FOR TODAY

PIETY

When I think about piety, the word "pious" often comes to mind. I envision individuals who proudly display their faith as if it were a badge, often projecting a critical or self-righteous image. I found it intriguing that piety is regarded as a gift from the Holy Spirit, particularly when the Bible frequently points out religious leaders who, despite their apparent devotion, failed to grasp the core of what truly mattered. These leaders often showcased their piety in public, especially during their interactions with Jesus, yet at times, it felt more like a performance than a sincere expression of faith.

Over time, I've learned that piety is a truly wonderful trait that has nothing to do with the shallow "pious" behavior I first mistakenly thought it meant. This unique and life-changing gift comes from the Holy Spirit and helps Christians grow in their faith and become more holy in God's eyes. Being religious doesn't just mean following rules or practices; true faith stems from having a deep relationship with the Holy Spirit. This authentic piety drives us toward a sincere and heartfelt devotion to God and those He has chosen.

This genuine expression of piety shapes our view of God as a sovereign Lord and, more intimately, a loving Father. It cultivates a relationship based on love and trust rather than fear or obligation. In Romans 8:14-15, St. Paul beautifully states, *Those guided by the Spirit of God are God's children. You did not receive a spirit of slavery to fall back into fear, but you received a spirit of adoption, through which we cry, "Abba, Father!"* This invitation to call God 'Abba, Father' reflects our deep belonging and acceptance within His family. The spirit of filial piety—a natural respect and love for our Divine Parent—grows within us.

Piety is a deep spiritual bond that encourages us to respect God's authority while embracing His generous love. It changes how we see the world and act by encouraging obedience that comes from love and gratitude. Being truly religious means lovingly obeying God throughout your life, not just because you have to. It changes how you think about your faith and lets you serve with real love, showing others the heart of our Father.

TAKE TIME TO:

- Reflect on your relationship with God and ask the Holy Spirit to guide you towards a deeper devotion, transforming your faith into an expression of love and gratitude.
- This week, focus on demonstrating your faith through acts of kindness, expressing genuine affection for God, and sharing the love of the Father with others. Your actions will reflect the profound gift of piety in your life.

SCRIPTURE VERSES TO READ AND REFLECT:

- Matthew 6:1-21
- Acts 3:12
- Hebrews 5:7

MY PRAYER FOR TODAY

OPENNESS TO THE HOLY SPIRIT

Being receptive to the Holy Spirit begins with dedicating time to sit in silence. Many people say they want to hear from God, but the real question is whether they make time for silence. Trying to have a conversation while surrounded by loud distractions makes it nearly impossible to truly listen. To truly hear what someone is saying, we must cultivate an environment of quiet and focus. This same principle applies to our relationship with God.

Today, many find it challenging to discern the Holy Spirit's guidance. The Holy Spirit often communicates in subtle ways, particularly during moments of silence, solitude, and relaxation. The Holy Spirit may unexpectedly reveal Himself during ordinary tasks when we are calm enough to listen. Through prayer, we can learn to hear His voice above the demands of our busy lives, though it requires practice. The Holy Spirit often communicates gently within our hearts, particularly in moments of quiet reflection. It's important to understand that His presence isn't summoned at will; instead, He tends to make Himself known unexpectedly, especially when we are undisturbed.

One effective way to open ourselves to the Holy Spirit is to set aside quiet time each day to pray and listen. I usually begin my prayers with praise and thanksgiving, reflect on my shortcomings, and seek God's forgiveness. Then, I read a Psalm and jot down any thoughts or insights that resonate with me during this time of prayer, asking the Holy Spirit for wisdom and clarity. I conclude my prayers with any petitions—either my own or those I have been asked to share in prayer.

However, being open to the Holy Spirit doesn't end here. Throughout the day, you may receive gentle promptings from the Lord, continuing the conversation begun in prayer. It's essential to stay receptive to His voice and be prepared to respond.

Commit to this practice of stillness as a way to nurture your spiritual well-being. As you cultivate this nurturing environment, you'll find your ability to discern God's guidance increases, leading to a deeper relationship with Him. Open your heart, welcome silence, and allow the Holy Spirit to transform your life—one quiet moment at a time.

Are you ready to begin? Set your intention today to make stillness a priority, and watch how the Holy Spirit reveals Himself in profound ways!

TAKE TIME TO:

- Begin your journey by dedicating time each day to sit in silence and open your heart to the Holy Spirit. In your busy schedule, carve out moments of quietness where you can be fully present.
- Start your prayer with gratitude, acknowledging the blessings in your life. Reflect on your day, seek forgiveness for your shortcomings, and invite the Holy Spirit into your heart. Read a Psalm, allowing its wisdom to resonate within you, and take note of any insights that arise during this sacred time. Conclude with your heartfelt petitions, leaving space for God to respond in His own time.

SCRIPTURE VERSES TO READ AND REFLECT:

- Proverbs 2:1-5
- John 14:26
- Revelation 3:20

MY PRAYER FOR TODAY

TRUST IN GOD

Have you heard of *discernment*? Discernment is the ability to hear from God and recognize His direction for your life. It's about seeking His guidance, understanding His will, and taking the next step. However, the crucial part of discernment isn't just hearing God's voice—it's trusting Him enough to take that next step.

So often, when we feel the tug in our hearts to move in a certain direction, we long for more clarity. We want to see the full picture before we act. But here's the challenge: God rarely shows us the entire roadmap. Instead, He invites us to step out in faith, trusting that He is leading us and will provide for us along the way.

This is where trust becomes a leap of faith. Many times, the next step God calls us into stretches us, pushing us beyond our comfort zone. Why? Because stepping into the unknown requires us to rely entirely on Him. If you're someone who craves control, this can feel overwhelming—but it's also an incredible opportunity to deepen your faith.

So, how do we trust in God when the way forward feels uncertain? Start by remembering all the ways God has shown up for you in the past. Reflect on His faithfulness, provision, and presence in times when you saw no way forward.

When doubt creeps in, shift your thoughts and words to align with God's truth. Speak life over your situation. Remind yourself *God is faithful. God is good. God is with me.*

Remember, trusting God isn't about having all the answers—it's about knowing *Who* holds the answers. Rest your thoughts on His promises, and declare His faithfulness with your words.

> *God is faithful. God is good. God is with me.*

TAKE TIME TO:

- Write down all the ways of God's past faithfulness. List answered prayers, breakthroughs, and unexpected blessings. When you're tempted to doubt, go back and read through these writings as a reminder that God has been faithful before and will be faithful again.
- Spend some time in prayer today and ask God what step He is calling you to take today that requires trust.

SCRIPTURE VERSES TO READ AND REFLECT:

- Proverbs 3:5-6
- Jeremiah 17:7-8
- Psalm 37:4-6

MY PRAYER FOR TODAY

THOUGHTS FOR THE WEEK

WEEKEND REFLECTION

SACRIFICE AND SURRENDER

The idea that we are called to give up something—whether it be time, comfort, or certain habits—serves as a reminder of the greater love and sacrifice made by Jesus. When we consider what He has given us, we look at our own lives and ask: What can I offer or change to grow closer to God?

As mentioned in the beginning, Lent provides us with an opportunity for self-reflection, repentance, and renewal. It encourages us to confront our imperfections and shortcomings, fostering a sense of humility. Surrendering our weaknesses doesn't imply defeat; instead, it allows God's grace to work within us. Our journey may involve struggles and setbacks, but it also offers a chance for us to deepen our relationship with God.

Fasting teaches us control and the ability to set aside our immediate desires, whereas almsgiving demonstrates our love for others, overcoming entitlement and self-absorption. Prayer is our direct line of communication with God, where we can express our concerns and seek His guidance and support.

In the end, the invitation to surrender and make sacrifices represents an opportunity for transformation. It requires us to let go of our preconceived ideas and remain open to God's intentions for our lives. As we embark on this Lenten journey, let us open our hearts to confront our flaws, rely on God's strength, and emerge as more compassionate and humble expressions of His love.

QUESTIONS FOR REFLECTION:

Read **Matthew 16:24–26** – What is God asking you to lay down or surrender this Lent?

Read **Isaiah 58:6–9** – How can you practice fasting in a way that aligns with God's heart for justice and mercy?

In what ways does this Scripture encourage you to align your priorities with God's will?

COURAGE

I was shy and timid when I was younger, often struggling to make even the simplest decisions. My desire to please others led me to seek their opinions, even though deep down, I knew what I truly wanted. I simply lacked the courage to stand firm and embrace what my heart was telling me.

When we have courage, we can be honest, kind, and fair while staying true to our faith in God. Without it, we may find ourselves swept away by the opinions of others, losing sight of who God created us to be. Courage allows us to make choices rooted in our values, even when those choices are challenging or unpopular.

Throughout history, countless missionaries have exemplified this courage, risking their lives for the Gospel of Jesus Christ. They faced persecution, hardship, and even death, yet they remained steadfast because they trusted in God's promises. Their bravery inspires us to live boldly for Christ, trusting that He is our strength and shield..

The importance of courage in living authentically and staying true to our convictions

Courage is not just about bold actions; it's about embracing our true selves and making choices that align with our values. It's about speaking truth with love, stepping out in faith, and trusting God's plan even when fear whispers doubts. The courage to live authentically is a testament to our faith in the Lord.

As we journey through life, let us remember the importance of courage in living authentically and staying true to our convictions. God calls us to be strong and courageous (Joshua 1:9 NASB), reminding us that we are never alone. He is with us, guiding and strengthening us every step of the way.

TAKE TIME TO:

- Who inspires you with their courage, and how can their example encourage you today?
- Spend time in prayer and recognize the areas in your life where fear has held you back from making authentic choices.
- How can you rely on God's strength to face your fears and stand firm in your convictions?

SCRIPTURE VERSES TO READ AND REFLECT:

- Joshua 1:9
- 1 Chronicles 28:20
- Deuteronomy 31:6-8

MY PRAYER FOR TODAY

CONFORMITY TO THE WILL OF GOD

St. Theresa of Avila, in her spiritual masterpiece *Interior Castle*, wrote, "The whole aim of any person who is beginning prayer—and don't forget this, because it is very important—should be that he work and prepare himself with determination and every possible effort to bring his will into conformity with God's will."[6] To be honest, the concept of aligning my will with the will of God is not easy! It is equivalent to relinquishing control, letting go of the steering wheel, and trusting God to take care of the situation.

There have been countless moments when I felt a divine nudge urging me to pursue a particular path. Yet, I often respond like a stubborn toddler, crossing my arms and declaring, "I don't want to!" I recall my niece during her childhood, shaking her head and insisting, "I am not listening, I am not listening," vividly reflecting my own resistance to God's guidance. How often do we mimic this same stance, resisting His plans in favor of our own?

Many of us set ambitious goals and encourage others to do the same, yet we often fail to consider whether these ambitions align with God's desires for us. The pursuit of spiritual growth requires vigilance and humility. A true spiritual teacher or coach will not simply offer advice but will guide you toward prayer, Scripture, and a deeper relationship with God as you seek the answers you need.

Surrendering my will to God is challenging. It requires letting go of my plans and trusting that His ways are higher and better than mine. But this surrender is a rewarding journey of faith and obedience. As believers, we are called to remember that our ultimate home is not in this world but with Jesus. Our goals and desires should align with this eternal perspective.

By actively seeking His guidance through prayer and Scripture, we can navigate life's challenges with a clearer vision. When we align our hearts and minds with His purpose, we live a more fulfilling and meaningful life that brings us closer to Him and prepares us for our eternal home.

TAKE TIME TO:

- This week, reflect on your ambitions, pray, and ask God for guidance. Write down thoughts, align goals with His will, trust the act of surrender, and watch life transform as you conform to His will.
- Seek out a spiritual mentor or friend to discuss surrender, align plans with God's purpose, and deepen faith through Scripture, prayer, and encouragement.

SCRIPTURE VERSES TO READ AND REFLECT:

- Jeremiah 29:11
- Romans 8:29
- Romans 12:2

MY PRAYER FOR TODAY

PURITY

*B*lessed are the pure in heart, for they shall see God* (Matthew 5:8 NIV). Purity is a way of living that flows from honesty, integrity, and aligning ourselves with God's will. It's about honoring the dignity of our bodies and keeping our hearts and minds fully devoted to Him. While purity often brings to mind sexual integrity, the Bible takes us deeper. True purity is about a heart and mind united in purpose and surrendered to God.[7] A divided heart only leads to confusion and frustration, but a heart focused on God reflects His purity and presence.

> *Purity begins with putting God first.*

Do you ever find yourself wavering in your decisions or commitments? I know I have—far more than I'd like to admit. I used to second-guess myself constantly, worrying about what others thought of me. But here's what I've learned: purity begins with putting God first. It means seeking His direction before making decisions and standing firm once we choose His way. Living out God's will isn't about pleasing others; it's about bringing delight to Him.

Sexual purity is part of this calling, but purity is for every area of life, no matter our age. It's reflected in what we say, what we listen to, what we watch, and even how we dress. Our choices should always honor God and point others toward Him. We're called to be encouragers, not stumbling blocks, helping our brothers and sisters live as righteous and pure followers of Christ.

As we navigate the complexities of life, it's crucial to remember that our commitment to purity can serve as a beacon of hope and truth. When faced with distractions or temptations, let's turn to Scripture and prayer to realign our hearts. Even in our most vulnerable moments, we can choose to lean into God and trust His guidance. Purity becomes not just a personal journey but also a communal effort; as we strive to embody this calling, we uplift one another, reminding each other of our shared purpose in Christ.

Moreover, pursuing purity means embracing grace—acknowledging that we will stumble, yet finding the strength to rise again through God's forgiveness and love. It's about cultivating a heart that consistently seeks to reflect Christ's character, allowing His light to shine in every corner of our lives.

TAKE TIME TO:

- Reflect on your choices and priorities. Are they aligned with God's will and reflecting His purity? Take a moment to pray for guidance and commit to living a life that honors Him in every aspect.
- Embrace the call to purity in your life—beyond just sexual integrity. Share your commitment with friends and family, and become a source of encouragement to others to help each other grow as righteous followers of Christ!

SCRIPTURE VERSES TO READ AND REFLECT:

- James 4:8-9
- 1 Peter 1:22-23
- Revelation 19:8

Purity is a way of living that flows from honesty, integrity, and aligning ourselves with God's will.

MY PRAYER FOR TODAY

SELF-CONTROL

As we navigate this journey of renewal and transformation, it's important to remember that it's not just about restraint; it's about cultivating an intentional approach to our thoughts and actions. Each time we choose to pause, reflect, and respond thoughtfully, we are not only honoring ourselves but also honoring God's purpose for our lives and the lives of those we love.

Self-control is like tending a garden. It requires diligence, patience, and understanding of what to nurture and what to pull out. We need to be aware of the weeds of impatience or anger that can grow quickly when we desire to intervene. Instead, we can choose to give understanding and kindness time to grow. Just like in gardening, the fruits of self-control can take time to develop, and we must be willing to trust the process.

In moments of temptation—when we feel the impulse to speak out or take control—let's take a breath and ask ourselves: "What does God want me to learn in this situation?" This simple question can shift our hearts and lead us toward grace-filled responses.

Moreover, practicing self-control doesn't mean we become passive; instead, we aim to actively engage in a prayerful stance, inviting the Holy Spirit into our interactions. By doing so, we become conduits of God's love and wisdom, open to what He is saying and how He is guiding us.

This week, let's challenge ourselves to embrace self-control in practical ways. Perhaps we can set aside a few moments each day to contemplate and ask for guidance on how to best respond in various situations—whether it's with our family, children, our friends, or even within ourselves. Remind yourself that it's perfectly okay to refrain from sharing your thoughts immediately. Allowing time and space for reflection leads to far deeper conversations and connections.

> *Allowing time and space for reflection leads to far deeper conversations and connections.*

As we explore this virtue together, let's also remind each other that we are not alone in this journey. Each one of us wrestles with the need for control, and sharing our struggles provides a rich tapestry of encouragement and community.

May our hearts be open to the transformative work the Lord is doing within us. Let's lean into self-control as an act of trust, honoring our Creator and growing into the righteous, joyful beings He created us to be. Together, let's embrace this challenge, knowing that with God's love as our foundation, we will cultivate self-control that reflects His grace and wisdom in our lives and the lives of those around us.

TAKE TIME TO:

- Set aside daily meditation and prayer for divine guidance, share your journey with trusted individuals, and grow in self-control and compassion to honor God's purpose in our lives.
- The next time you feel the urge to respond impulsively, take a moment to pause and ask yourself, "What does God want me to learn in this situation?" Allow this reflection to guide your actions and conversations.

SCRIPTURE VERSES TO READ AND REFLECT:

- Galatians 5:22-23
- 2 Timothy 1:7
- 1 Corinthians 10:13

MY PRAYER FOR TODAY

THOUGHTS FOR THE WEEK

WEEKEND REFLECTION

RENEWAL AND TRANSFORMATION

In my book *Restored*, I delve into the profound journey of rediscovering our true identity in a world where many of us often feel disconnected from our authentic selves. At the very essence of our being, we are children of God. However, in the complexities of modern life, many struggle to embody and live out this beautiful reality. Our imperfections and sins can cloud our perception, making us feel insignificant or unworthy in our own eyes and in the eyes of others.

Yet, in His boundless love and desire to restore humanity, God made the ultimate sacrifice by giving His only Son, Jesus. This act reveals the depth of His love and provides a pathway to renewal and transformation through His grace. The real challenge we face is in fully accepting and internalizing this fundamental truth: that God loves us so profoundly that He was willing to give everything, including His one and only Son, for our sake (John 3:16). Accepting this truth is essential to restoring our identity and reconnecting with the reality of who we are meant to be.

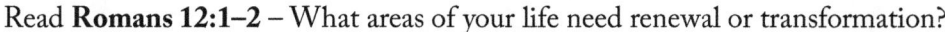

QUESTIONS FOR REFLECTION:

Read **Romans 12:1–2** – What areas of your life need renewal or transformation?

Read **Ezekiel 36:26** – How does God's promise of a new heart and spirit bring hope to you today?

What steps can you take to let the Holy Spirit renew your mind during this season?

PATIENCE

Why do I constantly feel rushed? In our busy lives, it often feels like countless demands and obligations are pulling us in every direction, creating an overwhelming sense of urgency to act immediately. But as I prayed at the start of this new year, I felt a gentle yet powerful nudge from the Holy Spirit—an invitation to pause and breathe. At that moment, I realized I didn't have to rush through every task or decision. That simple truth uncovered something deeper: I had been carrying so much anxiety, which was quietly stealing my joy and my patience.

Patience is often overlooked, especially in a world that thrives on instant results. But as I reflect on my own life, I see how impatience can lead to frustration, anxiety, and even a lack of trust in God's timing. St. Thomas Aquinas reminds us, "The one way to combat anxiety is to grow in trust in God's providential care for our lives."[8] It is reassuring to know that when we surrender our worries to God, we find the patience to wait for His perfect timing.

When prioritizing time with God, we learn to wait well, knowing His ways are always best.

Prayer is the key to cultivating patience. In those quiet moments, when we turn to God with our frustrations and hurried thoughts, we are reminded that His timing is never rushed. Carving out moments of silence for prayer is a way of saying, *"Lord, I trust Your plan more than my own urgency."* When prioritizing time with God, we learn to wait well, knowing His ways are always best.

Let's take a moment to reflect on the life of Christ. Jesus, even in the face of the greatest trials, demonstrated perfect patience. He never rushed, never panicked, but always trusted His Father's will. As we immerse ourselves in Scripture and draw inspiration from the saints, we begin to see that patience isn't passive; it's a virtue rooted in faith and trust in God's plan.

In the stillness of prayer, we become more attuned to the Holy Spirit's guidance. This attentiveness allows us to face life's challenges with grace, trusting God in both the waiting and the unfolding. As St. Francis of Assisi wisely warned, "By the anxieties and worries of this life, Satan tries to dull man's heart and make a dwelling for himself there."[9] Let's not allow anxiety to steal our patience and trust in God.

As we move through this year, let's make a conscious effort to slow down, breathe deeply, and practice patience. By prioritizing our time with God, we can experience the joy and peace that comes from living in His presence, free from the chains of anxiety and haste. Remember, God's timing is always perfect, even when we can't see the whole picture. Take things one step at a time, trusting that in His hands, all things will come together for good (Romans 8:28).

TAKE TIME TO:

- Take a moment today to pause and ask yourself: *Am I rushing through life, missing opportunities to trust God's timing?* Spend a few quiet moments in prayer, surrendering your anxieties and impatience to Him. Trust that His plan is unfolding perfectly, even when you can't see it yet.
- Commit to carve out intentional time for prayer and stillness each day. Use this sacred space to align your heart with God's will and practice patience. Let your prayer be: *"Lord, I trust Your timing and plan for my life. Help me to rest in Your peace as I wait on You."*

SCRIPTURE VERSES TO READ AND REFLECT:

- Romans 8:25
- James 1:3-4
- Ephesians 4:2

Prayer is the key to cultivating patience.

MY PRAYER FOR TODAY

FAITH

In John 20:29, Jesus reminds us of the blessing that comes from believing without seeing. In a world that often demands evidence and proof, our faith calls us into a deeper relationship with God—one that isn't dependent on what is visibly seen or understood. Think about the moments in your own life when you've sought tangible proof of God's presence. Instead of searching for signs, ask yourself: *How is God revealing Himself in the unseen details of my life?*

Our words hold incredible power. They can lift others up or tear them down, encourage faith, or fuel doubt. In times of uncertainty or struggle, what are you speaking into your life? Are your words rooted in faith? As Paul writes in 2 Corinthians 4:13, *Since, then, we have the same spirit of faith, according to what is written, "I believed, therefore I spoke," we too believe and therefore speak* (NABRE). Let your faith be reflected in what you say, shaping your own heart and the hearts of those around you.

Life doesn't always give us clear answers. In moments of doubt or confusion, it's easy to feel overwhelmed. But clarity comes when we lean into God's promises. Instead of simply asking for relief in prayer, consider asking God for direction and discernment. He cares about your questions, your fears, and your uncertainty. Invite Him into those moments, and trust that He will guide you.

Faith is more than just a feeling—it's an action. It's stepping forward even when you don't see the full picture. Think of the courageous women of the Bible—Hannah, Ruth, Mary. Each faced trials that tested their faith, but they chose to trust God and move forward. Hannah, desperate for a child, prayed for God's response. Ruth, a widow, followed Naomi's guidance, trusting in God's provision. Mary, chosen to bear the Savior, embraced her

> *Faith is more than just a feeling—it's an action.*

divine calling despite uncertainty. Their stories demonstrate that faith is not just about enduring hardship but about obedience and trusting in God's plan. What about you? Is there an area in your life where God is asking you to step out in faith? Take that step, knowing He walks with you.

As we navigate our daily lives, let's commit to nurturing our faith intentionally. Challenge yourself to speak words of faith and clarity that inspire hope and trust in God's presence. Remember, Jesus calls you blessed for believing without seeing (John 20:29). Embrace this gift fully, and let it shine in your life as a testimony to others.

TAKE TIME TO:

- Reflect on how God reveals Himself in the unseen details of your life. Set aside time this week to journal your thoughts. Write down specific instances where you felt God's presence, even when it wasn't evident.
- Take a moment to assess the words you speak over your life and the lives of others. This week, commit to speaking words that are rooted in faith, hope, and encouragement. Each day, choose a scripture or affirmation that resonates with you and incorporate it into your conversations and prayers.

SCRIPTURE VERSES TO READ AND REFLECT:

- Ephesians 2:8-10
- Hebrews 11:1-3
- 2 Corinthians 5:7

MY PRAYER FOR TODAY

HOPE

Micah 7:7 highlights the significance of hope, which goes beyond mere wishing; it embodies a profound assurance that something good will happen. This hope aligns with the intrinsic desire for happiness that God has placed within each of us. It motivates us to refine our intentions and steers us toward His Kingdom. In challenging times, hope serves as our lifeline, providing strength when we face isolation and allowing us to anticipate eternal joy while reminding us of God's unwavering faithfulness.

In my introduction, I shared how the loss of my first husband cast a shadow over my Lenten journey. That season felt overwhelmingly dark, yet there were moments when I still felt hope. Looking back, I realize that my increased time in Scripture and prayer was what sustained me. It was when I drew closer to God that I noticed my hope growing stronger.

Hopelessness often creeps in when we drift away from God. One of the most effective ways to reconnect is through Scripture—especially the Psalms. These genuine, heartfelt prayers demonstrate that even the psalmist felt despair and found courage in turning to God.

God is our rock and the foundation of our hopes and dreams, yet His timing can oftentimes be mysterious. The true test of hope often comes during times of hardship. Rather than becoming discouraged when things don't go as planned, we are encouraged to rest our souls in Him. We can rediscover hope by shifting our perspective from focusing on our problems to recognizing His blessings.

Titus 2:13 encourages us to hold on to the "blessed hope" of Christ's return, reminding us of the fulfillment of God's promises through Jesus. However, we must remember that Satan aims to ensnare us in hopelessness, knowing that despair can weaken our faith. When faced with trials, anxiety can overshadow our ability to recognize Jesus' presence in our lives, feeding our discouragement.

Hope invites us to rise above these challenges, encouraging us to trust in God's unwavering faithfulness and hold tightly to His promises. By centering our thoughts on His love and grace, we can find joy amid darkness, knowing that God's intentions for us are always good.

Lent is an opportunity to renew our commitment to Christ, deepen our trust, and awaken new hope. It's a season of healing as we become more aware of the Christ child being born anew in us. This Lent, let us slow down, reflect, and wait with open hands and expectant hearts. Let us look for Jesus in the good and difficult, the known and the uncertain, and hold onto the hope that He is always working for our good.

"You see, it is in the waiting that God is getting things in place for you."[10] (*Restored*)

TAKE TIME TO:

- This Lent, take a moment each day to immerse yourself in Scripture. Let the Psalms guide your reflections and prayers, fostering a deeper connection with God as you rediscover hope in His promises. Set aside distractions, silence your worries, and intentionally seek Him with an open heart.
- As we enter this season of renewal, make it a daily habit to express gratitude, reflecting on the many blessings God has already given you. Take a moment to write them down below.

SCRIPTURE VERSES TO READ AND REFLECT:

- Romans 8:25
- James 1:3-4
- Ephesians 4:2

MY PRAYER FOR TODAY

LOVE

As believers, we become sons and daughters of God through the profound grace of divine adoption, a gift we embrace by faith, through the waters of baptism, and the Spirit's transformative power. Those who receive this incredible blessing are not only wrapped in God's love and protection but are also empowered to extend that love to others, following the example set by Jesus. We are encouraged to align our hearts, hopes, and prayers with the Father through Christ. The Apostle Paul highlights our unique identity in his teachings on generations and God's covenant, emphasizing that our status as God's children is not merely a title—it's a profound reality stemming from our participation in His divine nature.

In 1 John 3:1, we read, *See what love the Father has bestowed on us that we may be called the children of God* (NIV). This passage serves as a powerful reminder of the extent of God's love for us. It's essential to recognize that God's love is not just an abstract concept; it's an active and creative force that calls us into a relationship with Him. This "calling" marks the beginning of an intimate relationship that can be beautifully illustrated by the bond between a parent and child. Through God's loving act of creation, we belong to Him as securely and unconditionally as children belong to their parents. The affirmation, "And that is what we are!" reinforces this intimate relationship—we are indeed children of God.

We are not merely invited to observe this love from afar but are encouraged to experience it within ourselves. As the Bible reminds us, God's love is not just something He displays; it is something He infuses into our very being. God created each of us in a unique manner; in fact, God made only one of you. You are distinct and unlike anyone who has ever existed or ever will. The reason you were intentionally created is that God desired someone like you and has divine plans for your life.

Perhaps you're feeling overwhelmed or worthless, weighed down by life's challenges. It may seem that you have endured more than you can bear, leaving you feeling as though you aren't worth much at all. But take a moment to reflect on God's words: *Because you are precious in my eyes, and honored, and I love you* (Isaiah 43:4, NABRE). God never describes His love in terms of material possessions like diamonds; instead, He proclaims His love for you.

> *You are important enough to Me to justify the death of My Son.*

David Eckman beautifully articulates this truth in his book *Becoming Who God Intended*, reminding us that God declares, "My Son is dying for you because you are worth a Son to Me." What a powerful truth! God sees your worth as so significant that He sent His Only Son, Jesus, to take your place and offer you the gift of eternal relationship with Him.

If you ever question your worth or feel lost and discouraged, remember that God views you through the lens of love. He declares, "You are important enough to Me to justify the death of My Son." This invitation is clear: God desires a close, intimate relationship with you.

So, why delay? Run to His arms and let Him speak those affirming words: "I love you. I love you." You might be wrestling with feelings of unlovability, thinking, "God, I don't feel worthy of such love." You may feel ensnared by guilt and shame, but today is the day to take a bold step of faith. Trust in His promise that you are precious in His sight.

TAKE TIME TO:

- Take a moment today to pause and reflect on your identity as a beloved child of God. Write a prayer or affirmation that celebrates your unique worth and divine purpose. Allow God's love to fill your heart and reshape your thoughts.
- Reach out to someone in your life who may feel overwhelmed or undervalued. Share the powerful truth of God's love and worthiness as expressed in Isaiah 43:4 and 1 John 3:1. Encourage them to recognize their significance in God's eyes.

SCRIPTURE VERSES TO READ AND REFLECT:

- 1 John 3:1
- Isaiah 43:4
- Colossians 3:14

MY PRAYER FOR TODAY

THOUGHTS FOR THE WEEK

WEEKEND REFLECTION

JESUS' JOURNEY TO THE CROSS

As we approach the celebration of Easter, I frequently experience profound unease. I cannot tolerate witnessing anyone endure suffering. I remember a particular experience when my stepdad had just undergone open heart surgery. I went to visit him in the hospital, and as soon as I entered the room, I was confronted with the sight of his exposed chest, complete with stitches and tubes. After the shock hit me hard, I got dizzy and broke out in a sweat. My mom quickly got me a chair, and at that moment, I realized that I couldn't offer her the support she needed.

This personal experience resonates with my dread of Jesus' journey to the cross. I think about the immense suffering He endured—not just for Himself, but for all of humanity. We are the reason He had to take that path. It is vital to recognize that even though Jesus is divine, Jesus embraced all of humanity, taking on flesh, blood, and the pain associated with suffering.

Through His journey, Jesus completely immersed Himself in our pain and agony. Thus, whenever we experience suffering, we can never say that He doesn't relate to our struggles; in fact, we understand that the exact opposite is true. In our moments of suffering, we can find solace in the truth that Jesus deeply relates to our experiences, having walked the path of suffering Himself.

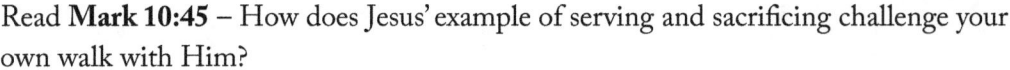

QUESTIONS FOR REFLECTION:

Read **Mark 10:45** – How does Jesus' example of serving and sacrificing challenge your own walk with Him?

Read **John 13:12–17** – How can you practice humility and serve others this Lent?

Read **Luke 22:39–46** – How does Jesus' prayer in Gethsemane shape your understanding of surrender to God's will?

JOY

As we enter the latter part of the Lenten season, we are called to contemplate the true essence of joy—one that goes beyond this world's fleeting pleasures and is anchored in Christ's Resurrection and His ultimate return. This joy is unlike anything found in worldly possessions, achievements, or circumstances; it flourishes in a relationship with God alone.

True joy transcends the fleeting happiness of earthly experiences and finds its true source in Christ. By shifting our focus to Him, we begin to understand that He is the only One who can fill the deepest longings of our hearts with lasting and complete joy. Henri Nouwen wisely reminds us, "Joy does not simply happen to us. We have to choose joy and keep choosing it every day. It is a choice based on the knowledge that we belong to God and have found our refuge and safety in Him, and that nothing—not even death —can separate us from His love."[11] Joy is not merely an emotion but an intentional choice rooted in our daily relationship with Christ—a decision we make in moments of celebration and struggle.

To rejoice is to express joy in recognition of God's endless goodness. The profound truth of John 3:16 resonates in our souls, *For God so loved the world that he gave his one and only Son, that whoever believes in him shall not perish but have eternal life* (NIV). This monumental gift of love and grace compels us to rejoice, awakening within us a desire to celebrate His unfailing faithfulness.

Even amid trials, we are called to rejoice—uniting our struggles with Christ's passion, recognizing that our suffering can bear fruit when we invite His presence into our pain.

This joy doesn't depend on what's going on in our lives; it's a fruit of the Holy Spirit that grows in our faith. We are reminded that God's love is the wellspring of our joy and that sharing this love is how we live out our faith authentically.

TAKE TIME TO:

- Reflect on the moments when you can invite Christ into your daily life, whether through prayer, scripture reading, or small acts of kindness. Keep a journal to document these moments of joy, noting how they arise from your relationship with God, even amidst challenges.
- Consider serving in a local outreach or mission, spreading the love of God and the joy that comes from knowing Him to those in need.

SCRIPTURE VERSES TO READ AND REFLECT:

- Nehemiah 8:10
- Psalm 16:11
- Romans 15:13
- John 16:22

MY PRAYER FOR TODAY

MEEKNESS

Today, let's reflect on the virtue of meekness—a misunderstood but profoundly transformative quality. In His Sermon on the Mount, Jesus imparts timeless wisdom through the Beatitudes, declaring, *Blessed are the meek, for they will inherit the land* (Matthew 5:5 NABRE).

At first glance, the world's definition of meekness might seem unappealing. According to Merriam-Webster, meekness is characterized by mildness, humility, or submission.[12] The Easton Bible Dictionary, however, paints a richer picture: meekness is a calmness of spirit, and a mind not easily provoked.[13] When I look around, I see how rare this virtue has become. In a world full of hurried conversations and reactions, meekness shines as a countercultural beacon, calling us to live with gentleness and intentionality.

A deep trust in God's timing and justice is at the heart of meekness. It's tempting to take matters into our own hands, fight for control, or seek immediate validation. But true meekness rests in the assurance that God is at work, even in unseen ways. When we surrender our battles to Him, we free ourselves from the weight of striving and find peace in His perfect will.

> *Meekness isn't weakness—it's power under control.*

Meekness isn't weakness—it's power under control. It calls us to temper strength with kindness in both our words and actions. In a culture where force and manipulation often seem like the quickest paths to success, meekness invites us to listen, seek understanding, and uplift others. By embodying gentleness, we create spaces of safety and compassion that reflect the heart of Christ.

A calm and composed spirit is the hallmark of meekness. Life's challenges can provoke frustration or anger, but meekness teaches us to respond with patience and grace. This doesn't mean ignoring difficult emotions—it means choosing not to be ruled by them. This is not always easy. When someone approaches us aggressively, our instinct is to reciprocate their behavior. However, practices like prayer, deep breathing, or pausing before reacting can help us reflect God's peace, even in tumultuous moments.

Meekness and humility walk hand in hand. Humility acknowledges our limitations and dependence on God while recognizing the value in others. In a world that celebrates self-promotion, humility reminds us that true greatness lies in serving others and pointing to God's glory. When we let go of the need to dominate or seek recognition, we make room for His power to work through us.

Meekness isn't about shrinking back or being passive—it's about living with quiet strength, confidence in God, and a heart attuned to the needs of others.

TAKE TIME TO:

- Take time today to pray and ask God to cultivate meekness in your heart. Commit to practicing one specific aspect of meekness—trusting God, gentleness, calmness, or humility—in your interactions this week.
- Choose one person in your life to bless through an act of gentleness or humility today. Whether it's through kind words, active listening, or an unexpected gesture of care, let your actions reflect the heart of Christ.

SCRIPTURE VERSES TO READ AND REFLECT:

- Colossians 3:12
- Titus 3:2
- Ephesians 4:2

MY PRAYER FOR TODAY

PRUDENCE

Do you enjoy taking risks? Personally, I wouldn't say I'm much of a risk-taker. Sure, I've made some quick decisions in the past that could've used a little more thought. But when it comes to taking big risks, I tend to hold back.

That said, let's talk about prudence—a word that doesn't get much attention these days. Sometimes, people might say, "Oh, you're such a prude," implying that someone's overly cautious or strict. But the true meaning of prudence is far more profound. It's about using wisdom, good judgment, and careful reasoning to navigate decisions and risks.[14]

Prudence is the ability to recognize what's truly good in any given situation and determine the best path to achieve it. A prudent person is intentional and always mindful of where they're heading. This virtue shapes how we think and act, ensuring our choices align with what's wise. Without prudence, bravery can slip into recklessness, mercy can be mistaken for weakness, and self-control can become an unhealthy obsession.

When life presents us with decisions, it's easy to act on impulse. But prudence invites us to pause and consider the consequences. St. Augustine said it beautifully: "*Patience is the companion of wisdom.*"[15]

Developing prudence takes time, but it's an essential part of living wisely and nurturing all other virtues. Take time to learn from your own experiences—and the experiences of others—and let prudence guide your steps.

TAKE TIME TO:

- The next time you're faced with a big decision, take a moment to reflect. Ask yourself: What is the wisest choice I can make in this situation? Let prudence guide your path.
- Commit to learning from your experiences and seeking wisdom daily. Spend time in prayer or reflection, asking God for the gift of prudence to navigate life's challenges with grace and clarity.

SCRIPTURE VERSES TO READ AND REFLECT:

- Proverbs 14:15
- 1 Thessalonians 5:21
- Proverbs 1:1-7

MY PRAYER FOR TODAY

JUSTICE

In a world often clouded by chaos and injustice, we are called to embrace justice—not just as an idea but as a way of life. Justice is our commitment to uphold what is right in how we relate to God and those around us. It's about living with fairness, empathy, and a heart anchored in truth.

Justice toward God begins with a deep reverence for who He is. It's recognizing His sovereignty and responding with love, gratitude, and obedience. When we honor Him with our worship and devotion, we align ourselves with His purpose, allowing His wisdom to guide us through life's complexities.

In our relationships with others, justice calls us to reflect God's love through respect and integrity. It challenges us to recognize the inherent dignity in every person, regardless of their background or circumstances. As Leviticus 19:15 reminds us, *You shall not do injustice in judgment; you shall not show partiality to the poor nor give preference to the great, but you are to judge your neighbor fairly* (NASB). Justice urges us to resist bias and let righteousness guide our judgments.

But justice isn't just about fairness— it's about action.

But justice isn't just about fairness—it's about action. It moves us to repair brokenness in our communities, build bridges of trust, and extend kindness in places where division or conflict may thrive. Justice equips us to be agents of peace and truth, living out the call to be the hands and feet of Christ. Through this, we help create a culture where equity and compassion flourish.

When we choose justice, we not only honor our calling but also inspire others to do the same. We advocate for those who are unheard, fight for what's right, and stand up for those who are overlooked. In doing so, we reflect God's redemptive love and contribute to His desire for a just world.

As Christians, let us boldly pursue justice in all we do. May we be known for our unwavering commitment to truth, compassion, and fairness, becoming reflections of God's heart and transforming the world around us for His glory.

TAKE TIME TO:

- Today, reflect on how you can embody justice in your relationships and interactions. Recognize the dignity in every person you encounter and consider ways to speak out against injustice within your community.
- Consider ways that you can engage in local initiatives that uplift the marginalized and promote equity. Whether it's volunteering, educating yourself, or standing up for those who cannot, your involvement can make a significant impact.

SCRIPTURE VERSES TO READ AND REFLECT:

- Isaiah 1:17
- Isaiah 61:8
- Proverbs 31:9

*Justice equips us
to be agents of
peace and truth.*

MY PRAYER FOR TODAY

THOUGHTS FOR THE WEEK

WEEKEND REFLECTION

HOPE AND RESURRECTION

I often wonder how non-Christians cope with the loss of someone they deeply love. What source of hope do they turn to when they don't share the belief in the Resurrection of Jesus Christ? For me, the assurance of eternal life for my loved ones carries me through such painful experiences. Death does not have the final say, and I am reminded that this world is not my final home.

I find immense reassurance in John 14:2: *In My Father's house are many rooms; if that were not so, I would have told you, because I am going there to prepare a place for you* (NASB). Jesus is our bridegroom, and He is preparing a place for us. This is a promise of a future filled with hope and belonging.

Reflecting on the immense suffering that Jesus endured for humanity deepens my appreciation of His Resurrection. He overcame death and returned to life—a powerful testament to the promise of renewal and hope. Because of His Resurrection, we, too, can hold onto the hope of life beyond this earthly existence. Through Jesus' victory over death, we find the assurance that our loved ones who have passed are not lost; rather, they are waiting for us in the eternal home He has promised.

Ultimately, it is this message of hope and resurrection that sustains me and many believers through times of sorrow. In facing the reality of loss, we can take comfort in knowing that death does not have the final word. Jesus' Resurrection is a beacon of hope, reminding us that love transcends mortality and that one day, we will be reunited with those we dearly love. This promise gives our lives profound meaning and guides us through the pain of separation with faith and hope.

QUESTIONS FOR REFLECTION:

Read **John 11:25–26** – How does this promise of eternal life give you hope during Lent?

Read **2 Corinthians 5:17** – What does it mean for you to live as a new creation in Christ? How does this Scripture encourage you to look forward to the joy of Easter morning?

WISDOM

Reflecting, I can see a tapestry woven with the threads of key and pivotal people who handed me their faith and wisdom. Had I not encountered these souls when I did, I truly wonder where I would stand today in my journey with Christ!

As a little girl, I remember countless afternoons spent at the kitchen table with my grandma. With cookies and juice by our sides, we would dive into deep discussions about the world and our faith. After countless heartfelt conversations, she would always chuckle and say, "Well, we didn't solve any world problems, but at least we tried." In those moments, she unknowingly imparted so much of her gentle, steadfast wisdom—that I wouldn't fully appreciate until years later when I became an adult.

God, in His infinite grace, bestows upon us the wisdom needed to discern what is right and best in our lives. Throughout the Bible, we come across a beautiful collection of wisdom literature, books (Job, Proverbs, Ecclesiastes, Wisdom, Sirach, Psalms and Song of Songs), designed to guide us through the complexities of our daily decisions. What a precious gift God has given us in these guidebooks!

Think about the times you've found yourself wishing for clarity—when decisions felt overwhelming, and you were left spinning your wheels, unsure of which direction to take. It is during these moments that the wisdom found in Scripture can become an anchor for our restless hearts. Just as my grandma's gentle words guided me, the insights in God's Word can illuminate our paths and remind us that we are not alone in navigating life's challenges.

Let us lean into this gift of wisdom, seeking it out in prayer and reflection. Let us be open to the lessons that come through conversations—both with the wise ones in our lives and through the timeless truths of Scripture. In embracing this divine guidance, we find direction and a deeper connection to the God who loves us. Together, may we cherish the wisdom imparted to us, honoring those who have shaped our faith as we continue our journey with Christ.

TAKE TIME TO:

- Reflect on the influential figures in your life and the wisdom they've shared. Take a moment today to reach out to someone who has impacted your faith journey. Share your gratitude for their guidance, and consider how their insights align with the teachings of Scripture.
- Feeling lost or overwhelmed? Turn to the wisdom literature in the Bible (Job, Proverbs, Ecclesiastes, Wisdom, Sirach, Psalms, and Song of Songs) and find clarity and direction. Dedicate some time for prayer and reflection today—ask God to reveal the insights you need for your life's decisions.

SCRIPTURE VERSES TO READ AND REFLECT:

- James 1:5
- Psalm 111:10
- Colossians 4:5-6

MY PRAYER FOR TODAY

DILIGENCE

I can be stubborn at times, but one trait that frequently outweighs my stubbornness is diligence. Unlike stubbornness, which often stems from pride, diligence is a godly characteristic. There have been moments when I've told my daughter that I appreciate her stubbornness, though I wish she'd direct it toward the good rather than against me!

Diligence has taught me that it's not about striving in my own strength but about faithfully persevering in God's purpose, even when the road feels long or uncertain. This quality has become my guiding force in following God's will, especially as a writer. When God called me to write *Rise Up Women of God*, I thought He had made a mistake—it wasn't something I had ever envisioned for myself. But through spiritual direction from my pastor, I realized I had been listening to the wrong voice, one rooted in fear, which was not God's voice at all. When my pastor challenged me to choose between listening to God or the voice of fear from the Evil One, the answer was clear: I chose God.

Diligence isn't about perfection; it's about persistence. It's about showing up every day, whether you feel equipped or not, trusting that God will use your willingness for His glory.

> *Diligence isn't about perfection; it's about persistence.*

Writing my first Bible study was an act of faith fueled by diligence, and that same diligence continues to guide me as I strive to serve God through my work.

This virtue teaches us that honoring God requires consistent effort, care, and humility. Diligence calls us to press on, even when the results aren't immediate or the journey feels challenging. It's about aligning our hearts with God's will and serving others purposefully, knowing that every small, faithful step brings us closer to His divine plan.

Let me encourage you: whatever God is calling you to do, pursue it with diligence. Trust Him to equip you for the task and lean into His strength as you go. It's in the day-by-day, moment-by-moment acts of faithfulness that He does His most profound work in and through us.

TAKE TIME TO:

- Reflect on your own journey and identify one area where you feel called to exhibit diligence. Write down practical steps you can take this week to pursue that calling with perseverance, trusting that God will equip you every step of the way.
- Commit to showing up daily, even in the small things, and trust that God is working through your faithfulness. Let diligence guide you as you align your heart with His will and serve others for His glory.

SCRIPTURE VERSES TO READ AND REFLECT:

- Galatians 6:9
- 2 Peter 1:10
- James 1:12

MY PRAYER FOR TODAY

LOYALTY

In my journey of friendship, I have always believed in being loyal—standing by my friends through the good, the bad, and the ugly. It's simply part of who I am. Yet, as time has passed, I've come to realize that some people I once thought would always be by my side have chosen to leave. This realization has brought me both surprise and sadness.

It's easy to assume that loyalty is a universal trait, but I've learned that not everyone shares the same commitment. I'm reminded of the poem *Reason, Season, Lifetime* by an unknown author. The poem beautifully illustrates how the people we meet come into our lives for different purposes—some for a specific reason, others for a season, and a few for a lifetime.

Understanding this truth can help guide us in our relationships.

> *True loyalty reflects God's character, for He is unwavering in His faithfulness to us.*

According to Merriam-Webster, loyalty is defined as "a strong feeling of support or allegiance."[16] In a biblical context, loyalty takes on a deeper meaning as steadfastness and commitment to others and to the church. A great example of this is found in the story of Jonathan in the book of Samuel. Jonathan displayed incredible loyalty as David's friend, protecting him from his own father, Saul, who sought to harm David.

This example teaches us that loyalty is not just about being there during the good times—it's about standing firm, even when it requires sacrifice or courage. True loyalty reflects God's character, for He is unwavering in His faithfulness to us.

In reflecting on these themes of loyalty, I recognize the importance of embracing the loyalty I can give, while also accepting the varying levels of commitment that others may offer. It reminds us that our ultimate example of loyalty comes from God Himself, who promises never to leave or forsake us.

By being kind and patient and maintaining a faithful presence that reflects God's heart, we can consciously show others how much He loves them. Let's be loyal not just in words but in action, standing by our friends, family, and community with unwavering support and grace. Yet, let's always remember that our loyalty must first be to God, seeking His will in how we love and serve those around us.

When loyalty feels one-sided or disappointing, let it be an opportunity to lean into God's faithfulness. He remains constant—the One who will never walk away. Let that truth inspire us to give our loyalty generously, trusting God to guide our relationships and heal our hearts when others fall short.

Let's be the kind of people who are remembered for our faithfulness, who stand firm through the storms of life, and who reflect the heart of our Savior in everything we do.

TAKE TIME TO:

- Reflect on your friendship journey and extend loyalty to those around you, mirroring God's faithfulness. Be present for friends, family, and community, demonstrating love and support. Reach out to friends in need this week, reminding them of your support.
- Evaluate relationships in your life, considering their purpose, season, and lifetime. Evaluate loyalty and pray for God's guidance in nurturing connections that honor Him. Release expectations and invest in relationships that reflect His purpose, being open to lessons each connection brings.

SCRIPTURE VERSES TO READ AND REFLECT:

- Proverbs 17:17
- John 15:13
- 1 Corinthians 13:7

Loyalty is not just about being there during the good times—it's about standing firm, even when it requires sacrifice or courage.

MY PRAYER FOR TODAY

GENEROSITY

Generosity is truly an outpouring of oneself for others. I often hear people describe someone as "a generous person," and my first thought is that they must be wealthy, freely sharing their financial resources with those in need. But as I journey through life, I've come to realize that generosity wears many hats; it manifests not just in financial abundance, but also in the precious sharing of our time and talents.

I will never forget a particular day at church when the annual collection appeal was made from the pulpit. I sat there, tense, my heart racing as I felt the weight of our financial situation. Being a stay-at-home mom in a one-income household meant that every dollar counted, and living paycheck to paycheck was our reality. As the Pastor spoke of the fundraiser's significance and the potential impact it could have on our church community, I felt a wave of anxiety. I could feel the increasing pressure to give financially, but deep down, I knew our circumstances would not allow it. Then came a moment of clarity that turned my apprehension into empowerment. The Pastor acknowledged the struggles of some families in the congregation, gently encouraging us that generosity isn't only measured by monetary contributions. He posed a question that changed everything for me: "Do you have time to spare or talents that could help us at the church?"

At that moment, I straightened my back, and a spark ignited within me. It was as if a light bulb had turned on. *Yes, I could offer my time!* I had talents that could contribute positively to our church community. Maybe it was helping with children's activities or assisting in organizing events. Whatever it was, I realized with joy that I had permission to be generous, even if it didn't involve money.

Generosity goes beyond our finances; it's about the love we pour into what we do. It's about the willingness to lift others up, to share encouraging words, to lend a helping hand, and to create spaces where everyone can flourish. Each act of kindness, no matter how small, carries a significant impact on the lives of those around us.

We often find ourselves juggling numerous roles and responsibilities, but let us remember that we can still be generous with our time and talents. We are called to share our hearts and uplift one another, no matter our circumstances. Isn't that a beautiful expression of generosity?

So today, I invite you to reflect on how you can pour yourself out for others, recognizing that the unique gifts, time, and treasures you have to give may be just what someone else needs. Let us be reminded that it's not only the financial contributions that matter but also the heart behind our actions that makes a difference. Generosity, in all its forms, can change lives—and best of all, it enriches the soul of the giver.

> *Generosity goes beyond our finances; it's about the love we pour into what we do.*

TAKE TIME TO:

- Take time this week to reflect on the unique gifts God has given you. How can you use those gifts to serve your church community? Whether it's through teaching, organizing, or lending a helping hand, trust that your contribution—no matter the size—can bring encouragement and hope to others.
- Don't let doubts or limitations keep you from stepping forward! Prayerfully consider how you can make a difference. Your time, talents, and treasures are valuable. God can use them in ways you never imagined to bless others and glorify Him.

SCRIPTURE VERSES TO READ AND REFLECT:

- Acts 20:35
- Matthew 6:21
- 1 Timothy 6:18-19

MY PRAYER FOR TODAY

THOUGHTS FOR THE WEEK

EASTER REFLECTION

LIVING IN THE LIGHT OF
THE RESURRECTION

He has risen! Easter celebrates the ultimate victory—Jesus' defeat of sin and death. It's the fulfillment of God's promise to redeem and renew us, offering us eternal life and a close relationship with Him.

For many of us, the Resurrection is more than a historical event; it serves as a powerful reminder that new beginnings are possible, even amidst our daily struggles, doubts, and challenges. Easter invites us to embrace the light of hope, grace, and joy that the Resurrection brings.

Take a moment to consider the women who were the first to witness the empty tomb (Luke 24:1-12). They arrived in sorrow, bringing spices to anoint Jesus' body, fully expecting to find a sealed tomb. Instead, they were met by angels who proclaimed, *Why do you look for the living among the dead? He is not here; He has risen!* (Luke 24:5-6 NIV).

Imagine their shock and awe—how their grief transformed into joy! The same power that brought Jesus back to life is alive and at work in your life today. The empty tomb stands as a testament that nothing is impossible for God.

The empty tomb stands as a testament that nothing is impossible for God.

So, what does the Resurrection mean for you?

- It signifies that your past does not define who you are. Through Christ, you are forgiven and made new.
- It assures you that hope never fades, regardless of how dark circumstances may appear.
- It confirms that God's promises are real, and His love for you is everlasting.

What does the Resurrection mean to you personally?

Is there an area of your life where you need God's resurrection power to bring new life and hope?

How can you live in the joy and freedom of Easter every day?

CONCLUSION

As we come to the close of this Lenten devotional, we are reminded that Lent is a sacred invitation to renewal and transformation. Throughout this journey of reflection, repentance, and intentional action, we have walked a path of self-examination and spiritual growth. By confronting our struggles and weaknesses, we have allowed God's grace to strengthen us, helping us rise above them and embrace the purpose He has placed within us.

This season has deepened our resilience and compassion, revealing that true sacrifice is not just about what we give up but about who we are becoming. Through our small yet meaningful acts of kindness and service, we have reflected the love of Jesus. Our time in prayer has drawn us into deeper intimacy with God, preparing our hearts to fully enter the joy of Easter.

As we look back on the insights and reflections from this journey, may we carry forward the essence of Lent in our daily lives. Let our hearts not only be ready to celebrate the Resurrection but also be committed to living out that joy with purpose. This sacred season calls us to be vessels of love and hope, shining Christ's light into the world around us.

As we step into the hope and renewal of Easter, let us hold fast to the transformation we have experienced. May the lessons learned and the grace received throughout this season continue to shape us, drawing us closer to Jesus and inspiring us to share His love with others. With hearts full of anticipation, may we boldly embrace the gift of new life, carrying the power of renewal beyond this season into all that lies ahead.

NOTES

1. Visitor, O. S., & Staff, O. S. V. (2000). *Catechism of the Catholic Church*. Usccb Pub.

2. humility. (2025). In *Merriam-Webster Dictionary*. https://www.merriam-webster.com/dictionary/humility

3. Warren, R. (2002). *The Purpose Driven Life: What on earth am I here for?* http://ci.nii.ac.jp/ncid/BA69271100

4. O'Brien, K. (2011). *The Ignatian Adventure: Experiencing the Spiritual Exercises of St. Ignatius in Daily Life*. Loyola Press.

5. Hahn, S. (2009). *Catholic Bible Dictionary*. National Geographic Books.

6. Teresa, S. (1979). *The Interior Castle*. Paulist Press.

7. Corbitt, S. (2017, August 29). *What Christ means by purity of heart*. Ascension Press Media. https://media.ascensionpress.com/2016/09/09/christ-means-purity-heart/

8. *St. Thomas Aquinas' wisdom for handling anxiety*. (2023, November 12). Aleteia — Catholic Spirituality, Lifestyle, World News, and Culture. https://aleteia.org/2023/11/12/st-thomas-aquinas-wisdom-for-handling-anxiety

9. Francis, S. (1964). Writings.

10. Fahey, Lisa, page 71 (2023). *Restored: A Journey from Ordinary to Extraordinary*.

11. Christensen, M. J., & Laird, R. (2017). *The heart of Henri Nouwen: His Words of Blessing*. Crossroad Publishing.

12. meekness. (n.d.). In *Merriam-Webster Dictionary*. https://www.merriam-webster.com/dictionary/meekness

13. *Meekness - Easton's Bible Dictionary online*. (n.d.). Bible Study Tools. https://www.biblestudytools.com/dictionaries/eastons-bible-dictionary/meekness.html

14. prudence. (2025). In *Merriam-Webster Dictionary*. https://www.merriam-webster.com/dictionary/prudence

15. CHURCH FATHERS: *On patience (St. Augustine)*. (n.d.). https://www.newadvent.org/fathers/1315.htm

16. loyalty. (2025). In *Merriam-Webster Dictionary*. https://www.merriam-webster.com/dictionary/loyalty

ABOUT THE AUTHOR

 isa Fahey is an author and speaker with over twenty years of experience working with youth, adults, and women in the Church. She is the author of *Rise Up, Women of God, A Scripture Study on 1 John and 2 John; Simply, A Women's Study on Ecclesiastes; Simply Advent; Just As You Are, How Your Testimony Can Impact People In Ways You Never Thought Possible;* and *Restored: From Ordinary to Extraordinary.*

All are meant to inspire, encourage, and empower readers in their journey with God. Lisa draws on real-life stories and moments with God to inspire and encourage others.

At the age of 21, Lisa lost her first husband, which forever changed her approach to God and His Word. Through her work, she shares how God helped her to grow and rise up as a woman of God, even during the trials of life.

Although "life is hard and messy," Lisa is able to show her readers through her Bible studies and books that the key to experiencing life completely is to follow their calling by serving God.

If this book has blessed you, please share the message with others by posting on social media using #simplylent

Website
www.lisafahey.com

Podcast
Lisa Fahey Ministry (Apple & Spotify)

Follow Your Call Coaching
www.lisafahey.com/follow-your-call-coaching

Facebook
Christian Professional Women On Purpose - Lisa Fahey

Instagram
lisafaheyministry

Publishing
farmhousepublishings@gmail.com

LISA FAHEY MINISTRY - PODCAST

SCAN ME!

@LISAFAHEYMINISTRY / WWW.LISAFAHEY.COM

OTHER TITLES BY LISA FAHEY

SIMPLY: A WOMEN'S BIBLE STUDY ON ECCLESIASTES

A six week study of Ecclesiastes. This book
of wisdom teaches us that living simply is the
secret to experiencing life to the fullest.

RISE UP, WOMEN OF GOD: A STUDY OF 1 JOHN & 2 JOHN

This six week study of 1 and 2 John are the ideal Epistles
to guide us through life's questions and confusing times.

SIMPLY ADVENT: A DAILY DEVOTIONAL
TO PREPARE THE WAY FOR JESUS

Advent helps us simplify the chaos by
preparing our hearts for Christmas.

JUST AS YOU ARE: HOW YOUR TESTIMONY CAN IMPACT
PEOPLE IN WAYS YOU NEVER THOUGHT POSSIBLE

Your testimony can reach people for Christ
in ways you never thought possible.

RESTORED: FROM ORDINARY TO EXTRAORDINARY

Becoming the person God intended
you to be... Extraordinary